Dear Parent:
Your child's love of reading starts here!

Every child learns to read in a different way and at his or her own speed. You can help your young reader improve and become more confident by encouraging his or her own interests and abilities. You can also guide your child's spiritual development by reading stories with biblical values and Bible stories, like I Can Read! books published by Zonderkidz. From books your child reads with you to the first books he or she reads alone, there are I Can Read! books for every stage of reading:

SHARED READING
Basic language, word repetition, and whimsical illustrations, ideal for sharing with your emergent reader.

BEGINNING READING
Short sentences, familiar words, and simple concepts for children eager to read on their own.

READING WITH HELP
Engaging stories, longer sentences, and language play for developing readers.

READING ALONE
Complex plots, challenging vocabulary, and high-interest topics for the independent reader.

ADVANCED READING
Short paragraphs, chapters, and exciting themes for the perfect bridge to chapter books.

I Can Read! books have introduced children to the joy of reading since 1957. Featuring award-winning authors and illustrators and a fabulous cast of beloved characters, I Can Read! books set the standard for beginning readers.

A lifetime of discovery begins with the magical words **"I Can Read!"**

Visit www.icanread.com for information on enriching your child's reading experience.
Visit www.zonderkidz.com for more Zonderkidz I Can Read! titles.

Be strong and courageous. Do not be afraid
or terrified because of them, for the Lord
your God goes with you; he will never leave
you nor forsake you.
—*Deuteronomy 31:6*

ZONDERKIDZ

The Princess Twins and the Puppy
Copyright © 2011 by Mona Hodgson
Illustrations © 2015 Julie Olson

Requests for information should be addressed to:

Zonderkidz, 3900 Sparks Dr. SE, *Grand Rapids, Michigan 49546*

This edition: ISBN 978-0-310-75064-2 (softcover)

This edition: ISBN 978-0-310-75312-4 (hardcover)

Library of Congress Cataloging-in-Publication Data

Hodgson, Mona Gansber, 1954–
  The princess twins and the puppy / by Mona Hodgson.
    p. cm. — (I can read!)
  Summary: When the princesses' puppy runs off, Abby asks Jesus to help her be brave so she can go into the basement to search for the missing pet.
    ISBN 978-0-310-72709-5 (softcover)
  [1. Princesses—Fiction. 2. Twins—Fiction. 3. Sister—Fiction. 4. Dogs—Fiction. 5. Christian life—Fiction.] I. Title
  PZ7.H6649Psp 2012
  [E]—dc22   2010052443

Editor: Mary Hassinger
Art direction & design: Jamie DeBruyn

Printed in China

---

15 16 17 18 19 20 /DHC/ 7 6 5 4 3 2 1

ZONDERkidz

I Can Read!

BEGINNING 1 READING

The Princess Twins
and the Puppy

Story by Mona Hodgson
Pictures by Julie Olson

Princess Abby and her sister, Emma,

sipped tea in the garden.

Tickle. Tickle.

Something tickled Abby's leg.

Abby giggled and she wiggled.

Tickle. Tickle.

Abby looked under the table.

Puppy barked and jumped.

"It's not playtime,"

Emma told Puppy.

Tickle. Tickle.

"Shoo." Abby clapped her hands.

Puppy ran out of the garden.

Abby and Emma finished their tea.

Now it was playtime.

"Puppy," Princess Abby called.

"Puppy," called Princess Emma.

Puppy didn't come.

"Maybe Puppy ran up the tower,"
said Abby.

The princesses looked in the tower,

but they didn't find Puppy.

Abby opened the castle door.

"Puppy," she called.

Abby looked in Puppy's bed,

but she didn't find Puppy.

"Puppy," Princess Emma called.

Emma looked in her bedroom,
but she didn't find Puppy.

"Puppy," Princess Abby called.

She looked in the library,

but she didn't find Puppy.

Emma stopped at a closed door.

"What if Puppy is in the basement?"

she asked.

"Puppy," Abby called.

"Woof. Woof," said Puppy.

Princess Abby and Princess Emma

looked into the basement.

"Puppy!" they called.

Puppy didn't come.

"Woof. Woof," said Puppy.

"Puppy needs us," said Abby.

"I'm not going down there,"
Emma said.

Abby was afraid of the dark.

Abby had to be very brave.

"Jesus, help me be brave,"

prayed Abby.

Abby took a lantern.

She tiptoed down the stairs.

Abby's knees shook.

"Jesus is with me," she said.

"Woof. Woof," said Puppy.

Abby found Puppy stuck in a box.

Tickle. Tickle.

Abby tickled Puppy's chin.

"Thank you, Jesus, for making
me brave," prayed Abby.

Abby carried Puppy upstairs.

Puppy woofed and wiggled.

Now it really was playtime.